COUNT DRAWCULA'S
CARTOON FUN

How to draw brilliant beasts, baddies & bogeymen!

Frank Rodgers

André Deutsch Children's Books

Look out for
ANIMAL ART
CARTOON FUN
COMIC FUN
also by Frank Rodgers

Scholastic Children's Books,
7-9 Pratt Street, London NW1 0AE, UK
A division of Scholastic Publications Ltd
London~New York~Toronto~Sydney~Auckland

First published by Scholastic Publications Ltd, 1995

ISBN: 0 590 54193 5 (hb)
ISBN: 0 590 13357 8 (pb)

Typeset by Rapid Reprographics
Printed in Hong Kong

10 9 8 7 6 5 4 3 2 1

CONTENTS

Count Drawcula Welcomes You . . .

Hello everyone!
My name is Count Drawcula.
Welcome to my bat-infested studio.
I would like to take you around my castle,
introduce you to a few of my ghoul-friends
and show you how to draw some of my
favourite baddies – monsters, witches,
dragons, wolves, giants and, of course, the
best baddy of all . . . ME!
First of all, allow me to present some
members of my wonderfully revolting
family:

Mummy and Daddy

Granny and Grandpa

Uncle Clott and Aunt Plasma

and my wife Jugula with Drawcula Junior.

I painted these myself.
Good, aren't they?
My favourite, naturally, is this
gorgeous self-portrait . . . of ME!
Wouldn't you like to be able to
draw and paint faces as knobbly
and disgusting . . . I mean noble
and distinguished . . . as these?
Of course you would!
So come with me . . . if you dare!

Festering Features

As far as I am concerned, the most interesting cartoon characters to draw are BADDIES. Weird, wonderful, creepy, ugly baddies with faces like ham-and-pineapple pizzas or explosions in a dung heap. Yes – faces with character!

Not namby-pamby, sugar-sweet faces like these . . .

These are GOODIES' FACES . . . cheerful, decent, hopeful faces. Nice faces . . . DULL FACES! Not a wart, fang, slobber or spot in sight. Useless!

Just compare that lot with this deliciously disgusting collection of baddies showing off their FESTERING FEATURES!

Baddies need features they can be proud of. Take noses, for example.
If you drew a baddy with a nose like a button, it might not look nasty enough.
So, use your imagination. Give it a nose like . . .

a squashy tomato . . .   the point of a rocket . . .   or a boxing glove.

Now, isn't that just right? Of course it is!
Yes . . . give me a lumpy face, a hairy face or a creepy face any day.
Here's how to create your own instant baddy. Magnificently monsterish!

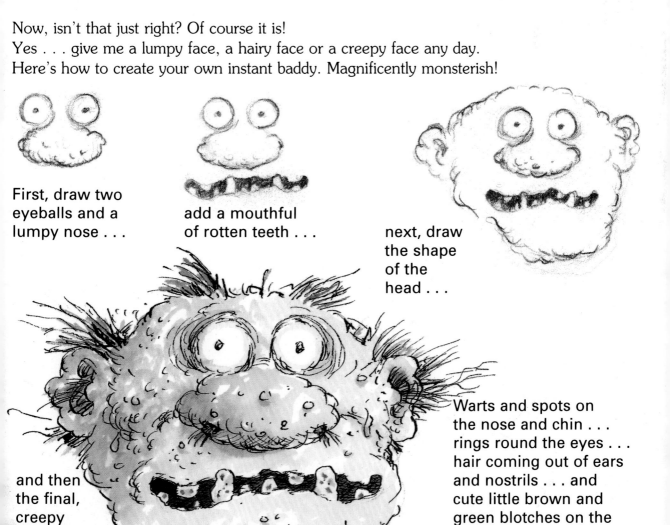

First, draw two
eyeballs and a
lumpy nose . . .

add a mouthful
of rotten teeth . . .

next, draw
the shape
of the
head . . .

and then
the final,
creepy
details . . .

Warts and spots on
the nose and chin . . .
rings round the eyes . . .
hair coming out of ears
and nostrils . . . and
cute little brown and
green blotches on the
yellow teeth.

Baddies in the News

Most people have played the game of horribilizing photographs in newspapers, haven't they? If you haven't, it's easy . . . and good practice for drawing your own revolting characters.

Use a fine-tipped black fibre pen and draw *lightly*. Practise at the edge of the paper by making delicate sweeping lines or clusters of small dots to try and create tones.

Once you've got the hang of it, try and blend in your changes to make the person look as if he or she was *photographed* that way!

This kind of thing is a bit too obvious . . .

and NOT very funny!

Here's a non-horribilized newspaper photograph. Try changing it slightly . . . so that the next person to read the newspaper doesn't notice at first, then does a double-take!

You could just alter the eyes . . .

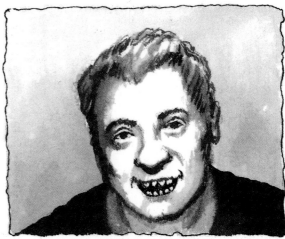

or the mouth . . .

or the nose . . .

or you could go for it and alter the whole face!

Warning: Sometimes such alterations can cause annoyance in a family . . . especially if you have horribilized a favourite politician, a model or a pop star. But then, that's part of the fun, isn't it?

Design Your Own Disgustingness

Now I'd like to show you the little 'designer' touches that I've added to my castle. Like these swathes of thick cobwebs draped between the pillars in the hall.

You can achieve a cobweb effect this way: first, paint the background; then, when it's dry . . .

use soft chalk or crayon to make the cobwebs by drawing sweeping curves connecting the pillars and arch.

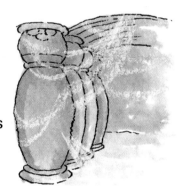

Cobwebs, of course, look wonderful set against blotchy, fungus-covered walls . . .

Just dampen the paper slightly, then use watered-down colours so that they spread and mingle at the edges . . .

then add little blotches of colour. Opposites are good for this . . . purple and yellow, red and green.

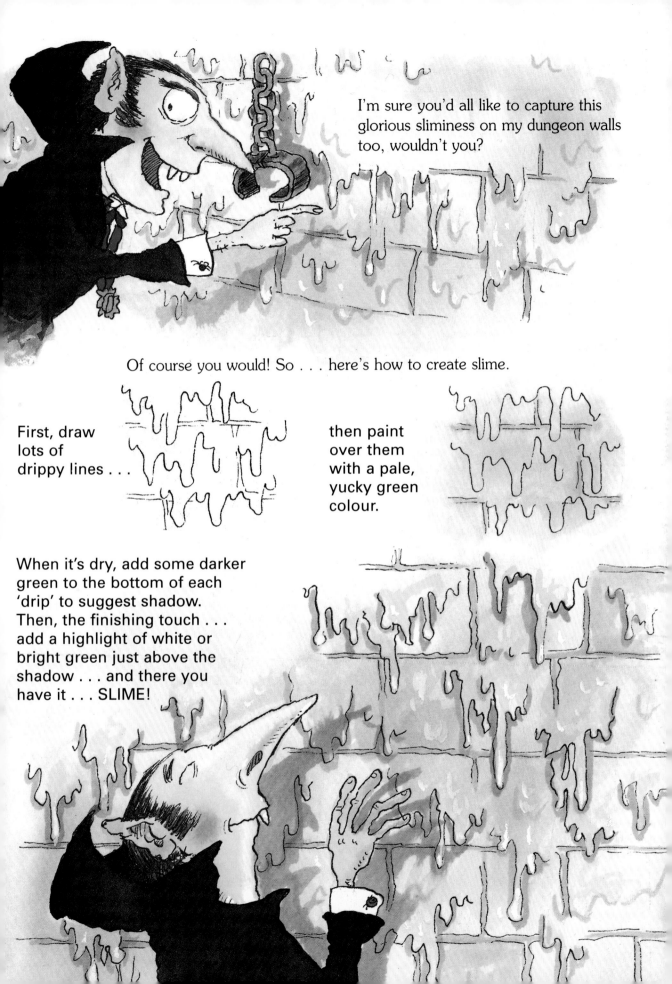

I'm sure you'd all like to capture this glorious sliminess on my dungeon walls too, wouldn't you?

Of course you would! So . . . here's how to create slime.

First, draw lots of drippy lines . . .

then paint over them with a pale, yucky green colour.

When it's dry, add some darker green to the bottom of each 'drip' to suggest shadow. Then, the finishing touch . . . add a highlight of white or bright green just above the shadow . . . and there you have it . . . SLIME!

Perfectly Creepy Pets

My castle is a real home . . . and, like lots of real homes, it is full of pets. Of course, my pets are not cuddly-wuddly, icky-type pets like bunnies, doggies, pussies, guinea-piggies or hammies . . . oh, no. My pets are ugly-bugly-type pets . . . bats, rats, spiders and cute little cockroaches.

Here's how to draw them. Remember always to sketch the outline with a pencil first, then 'ink in' over the top.

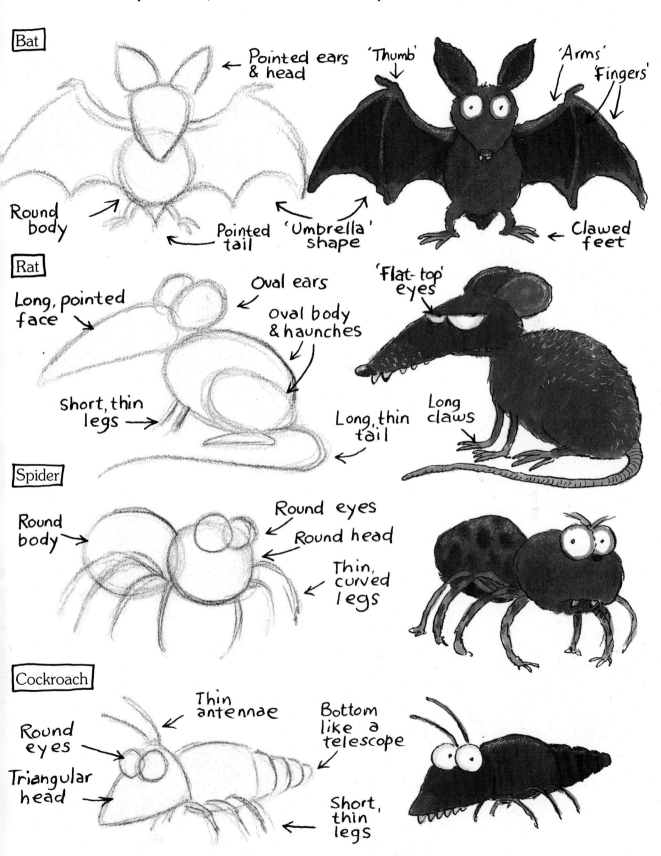

Bat
Pointed ears & head →
'Thumb'
'Arms'
'Fingers'
Round body
Pointed tail
'Umbrella' shape
Clawed feet

Rat
Oval ears
'Flat-top' eyes
Long, pointed face
Oval body & haunches
Short, thin legs →
Long, thin tail
Long claws

Spider
Round eyes
Round head
Round body →
Thin, curved legs

Cockroach
Thin antennae
Bottom like a telescope
Round eyes
Triangular head
Short, thin legs

Beasts and Bogeypersons

There are others who creep around my castle, keeping to the shadows, living in abandoned rooms . . . Behind this door lives the Beast. I've known him for about three hundred years, so he's a very old friend. Not only that, he's one of the ugliest people I know. Here's how to draw him.

mnngrghhrr... UGLY ?? ME? why, thank you!

Tapering head, flat chin & flat top

High shoulders

Wide, turned-down mouth with large tusks

Long, trailing arms

Large, 'sausage' fingers

Short legs

Big 'banana' feet

14

And these are the Bogeypersons.
Sneaky, creepy and furtive,
they love to jump out
of hiding and try to
scare me to death.
This, of course,
is very difficult as
I am dead already!

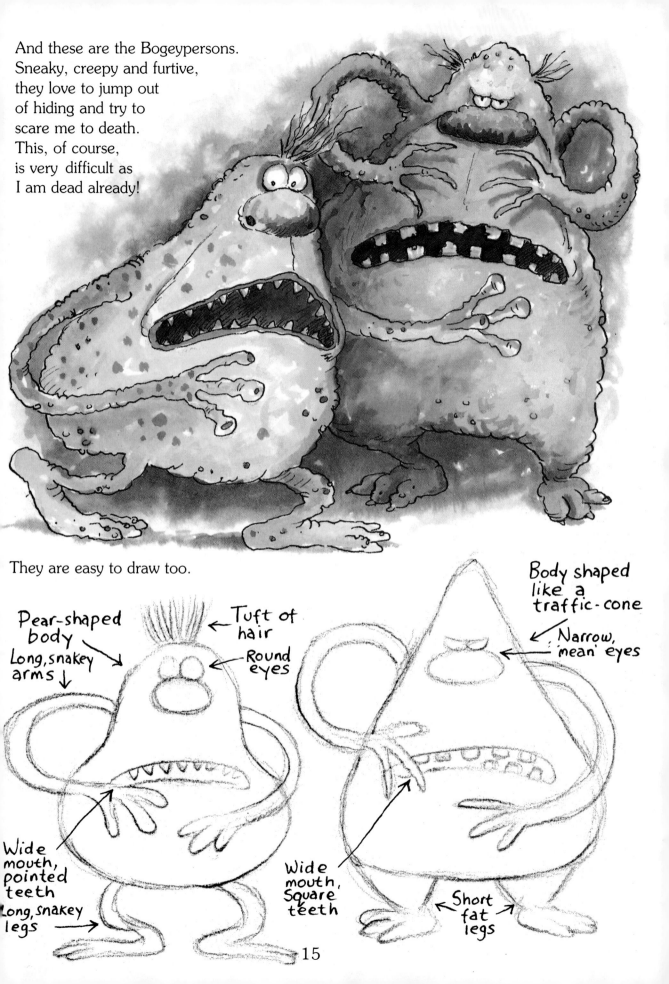

They are easy to draw too.

Pear-shaped
body
Long, snakey
arms

Tuft of
hair

Round
eyes

Body shaped
like a
traffic-cone

Narrow,
mean eyes

Wide
mouth,
pointed
teeth

Wide
mouth,
square
teeth

Long, snakey
legs

Short
fat
legs

15

Ghosts, Ghouls and Gargoyles

Here we are on the battlements of my castle under a marvellous howling moon. (That's what my friends the wolves call it.) Do you like my gorgeously grotesque gargoyles? I designed them myself.

Have a go at drawing your own. Remember, the more revolting the face, the better. Use bulging eyes and huge noses and nostrils. (Nose-picking and mouth-pulling add a touch of class!)

Large, round eyes →

Nose like old potato

Wide, down-turned mouth

pointed tongue

Triangular head

Or, if you like . . . copy my designs.

In the grounds I have all the things any self-respecting vampire needs for a beautiful garden: dead trees, a swamp, a ruined church and a mouldering graveyard.

Old tombstones are very interesting things to draw. They usually have nice designs on them featuring death's heads and skeletons.

I sketched these in my own graveyard, so why not pay a visit to one near you and draw the tombstones there? It'll be so quiet – no one will disturb you during the day . . . but watch out at night . . .

Skull shaped like a light-bulb

Neck & Collar-bone like a Coat-hanger

Pelvis like an old clock-key

Thigh like bone on pirate flag

Triangular feet with boney toes

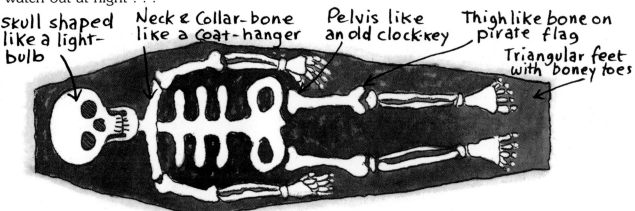

. . . you might find yourself with a real skeleton to draw!

A graveyard is such a nice place at night, especially under a howling moon. A delightful thing to illustrate!

Begin by doing a drawing like the one below. The moon is the source of light, so the lines of the shadows will radiate from it.

If you do your drawing on grey paper then this can act as the background tone. Then mix up three other tones in your paint tray – grey, white and black. Paint the surfaces of the tombstones that face the moon white, paint the parts that are not lit by the moon grey and, finally, paint the shadows black.

My graveyard is busy after dark. That's when the ghouls and ghosts come out.

Ghouls are a bit like mobile gargoyles. They're hideous creatures that creep out of their crypts or slither out of their sarcophagi to snare the unwary! Very nice people, actually. I've got a lot of ghoul-friends.

Do you remember how to paint slime? If you do, it will help you to paint a convincing ghoul. Once you've drawn its drippy, creepy face, just add the slime effects the way I showed you.

Ghosts are a little bit different from ghouls. There's not a lot *to* them – they're a bit *transparent* if you see what I mean. They float about graveyards wailing and groaning and gnashing their teeth. It's like music to my ears!

To create this ghost, first draw a few tombstones and colour with dark pencils or paint. Then use soft white chalk lightly to draw and fill in the shape of the ghost.

Creatures of the Night

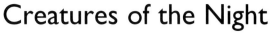

O ut there in the night, in the dark forests and lonely mountains, are some of my neighbours – goblins, vampires, trolls, werewolves and tree monsters . . . all fun to draw.

Goblins live in dark tunnels underground. They are sly, cunning and treacherous . . . my kind of people!

Large eyes →

← pointed ears

← Large, round head

Small, round body

Long, thick arms

Short legs

Vampires, of course, can change shape, so to make sure they take people by surprise they sometimes use unusual disguises . . .

vampire sheep . . .   vampire teddy . . .   vampire mop.

So, watch out if you're in the country, in a toyshop, in the kitchen . . . or anywhere. There could be vampires about!

Trolls are big, lumbering creatures that come from the deepest recesses of the earth and look a bit like volcanoes on legs.

Big ears

pointed head

'Volcano' shaped body

Wide mouth

Thick arms

Lumpy skin

Colour and texture of mossy stone

(Baby troll blowing its top!)

short, thick legs

Notice that a baby troll's head is larger in proportion to its body than an adult troll's head. (This is true of *all* babies.)

← Head almost half the size of the body →

Trolls only appear at night because, if caught by the rays of the sun, they are instantly turned to stone. As you can imagine, they don't go in much for beach holidays. (I can't say I'm very fond of the sun myself . . . it turns me to dust!)

Don't vacuum up that pile of dust, Mum... it might be *DAD!*

21

There are certain people . . . ordinary, uninteresting people who, when the full moon shines, become extraordinary and interesting! Of course . . . I'm talking about werewolves!

First, a few hairs start to sprout . . .

then ears shoot up . . .

the teeth become fangs . . .

the face changes shape . . . and someone who looked like a goofy goody becomes a brilliant baddy!

My night-class students are in for a big SURPRISE!

Like people who become werewolves, tree monsters appear rather harmless to begin with. They look just like . . . well, trees, actually. But under the right circumstances, the bad sap starts to rise and an ordinary elm or beech can become a tree monster!

First, draw part of the tree-trunk in the centre of the page.

Then make the wrinkles of the bark look like a face. (The nose could be a small branch.)

Next, draw branches like arms with long, twiggy fingers sprouting out on either side . . .

Give it a crop of twiggy hair and, finally, make the roots look like giant, gnarled feet. Now your tree monster is ready to stomp off and snare the unwary!

Fairy Tale Terrors

At dawn, tucked up in my cosy coffin, I like to settle down and read a fairy story. Do you know why? Well, it's because they have the most wonderfully, revoltingly rotten baddies in them – some of the best baddies ever to come out of books. Witches, wolves, giants, bears and wicked queens! Great characters!

Take giants, for instance. Cormoran, a giant in the story *Jack the Giant Killer*, had such a big appetite he could eat twenty cows washed down by a dozen barrels of beer. He could probably have flattened a building with one enormous burp! Imagine the size of the indigestion tablet he'd have needed after that! (In the end he didn't need one because Jack chopped off his head.) Ouch! Disgusting! Unfair to giants!

Giants were also ugly . . . and proud of it! Here is a charming line-up from their annual Ugly Contest. Have a go at copying them . . . or draw your own.

Not fair! You've got two more chances of winning than I have.

Blunderbore

Cyclops

The Red Etin

Horrible hair-do →

Evil eye

Nasty habit

Rotten teeth

Bad breath →

Witches are beautifully ugly too. Here's a portrait of one, pointing out all the best features.

Witches didn't usually get their heads chopped off but some of them came to a bad end. For instance, the witch in *Hansel and Gretel* was given a hot time of it in her own oven. Here she is before she ended up as a toastie.

Use triangles for all the rough shapes...

Hat →

Nose

Arms

← Face

Body →

Goldilocks and the Three Bears is a very old fairy story. When it was first told, hundreds of years ago when I was just a boy, the bears were *real* baddies . . . they *ate* Goldilocks!

This is how they looked then.

Clawed hands

Curved ears

Round head

Pointed nose

Thick tapering arms

Round, fat body

Short, thick legs

Unfortunately, over the years they had a personality change . . . they turned soft. Instead of scoffing Goldilocks, they just scared her away.

This is how they look now. Sad, isn't it?

Luckily, wolves haven't changed much in fairy stories. They've been bad for nearly a thousand years. As long ago as 1023 there was a story about wolves who scoffed a little girl in a red cap.

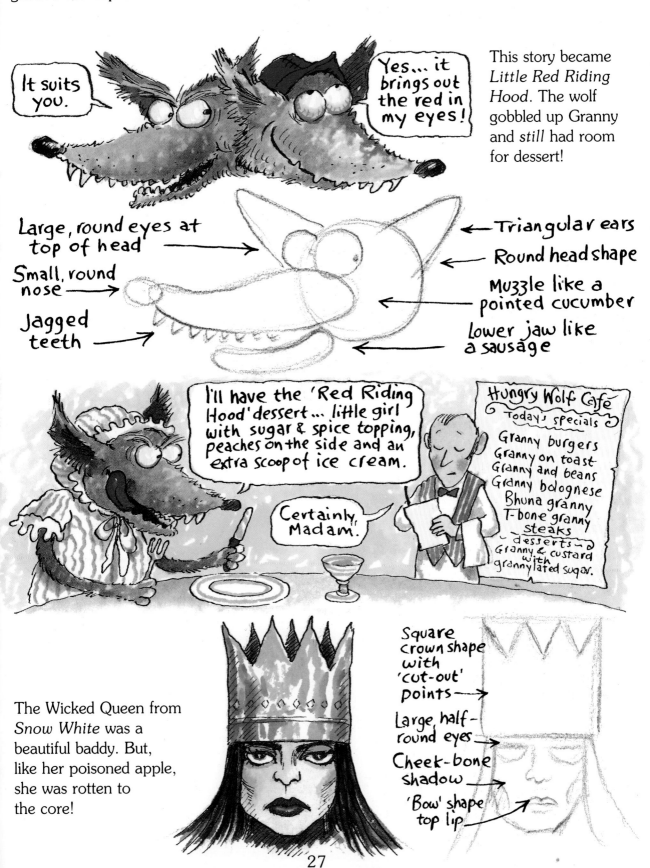

It suits you.

Yes... it brings out the red in my eyes!

This story became *Little Red Riding Hood*. The wolf gobbled up Granny and *still* had room for dessert!

Large, round eyes at top of head

Small, round nose

Jagged teeth

Triangular ears

Round head shape

Muzzle like a pointed cucumber

Lower jaw like a sausage

I'll have the 'Red Riding Hood' dessert... little girl with sugar & spice topping, peaches on the side and an extra scoop of ice cream.

Certainly, Madam.

Hungry Wolf Café
Today's specials
Granny burgers
Granny on toast
Granny and beans
Granny bolognese
Bhuna granny
T-bone granny steaks
~desserts~
Granny & custard with granny lated sugar.

The Wicked Queen from *Snow White* was a beautiful baddy. But, like her poisoned apple, she was rotten to the core!

Square crown shape with 'cut-out' points

Large, half-round eyes

Cheek-bone shadow

'Bow' shape top lip

27

Evil Aliens and Androids

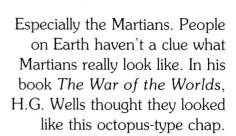

B addies, of course, are not restricted to this planet. Sometimes I have visitors from Outer Space. You'd be amazed at the number of downright rotten aliens there are out there.

Especially the Martians. People on Earth haven't a clue what Martians really look like. In his book *The War of the Worlds*, H.G. Wells thought they looked like this octopus-type chap.

While most people think they are little green creatures.

But they're all wrong . . . because Martians actually look like this. That's right, just like YOU! Imagine if they came to Earth to live . . . your best pal might be a Martian and you wouldn't know it!

Civilization in other galaxies is so advanced that most of the drudgery of life is done by androids . . . washing-up, vacuuming, tidying, homework etc. There are so many android spare-part shops that aliens like to build their own robots. So do I . . . by playing a little drawing game. I draw lots of different robot parts, cut them out and assemble them into complete androids. It's fun! Why not try it?
I've drawn a few spare parts to get you started.

Heads...   arms...   bodies...   legs...

There are robot baddies, of course . . . Here's quite a good-looking example.

But here's a cut-away drawing to show that beauty is really only skin-deep!

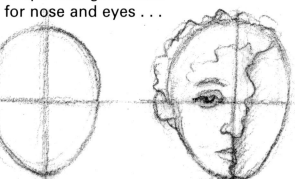

This is how to draw your own human/android.

Start with an oval shape with guidelines for nose and eyes . . .

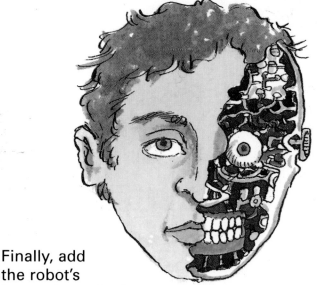

then draw the cut-away shape and fill in the human features.

Finally, add the robot's internal mechanism.

Story-book Baddies

This is my library. It is full of books that contain the most excellent baddies in literature. My favourite book is *Dr Jekyll and Mr Hyde*, because I thought that the change did Dr Jekyll such a power of good!

Ah! Tha bette

Professor Moriarty, Sherlock Holmes' arch-enemy, is another of my favourites. A brilliant brain and such good taste in clothes . . . just like me!

Small shoulder cape

'Chimney' shape

curved brim

Chin almost meets nose

Body shape like a traffic cone

Like me too, a lot of story-book baddies live in castles. Huge, dark, crumbling piles surrounded by icy moats and filled with the groans of the prisoners languishing in the dank dungeons. Ah, what a lovely, cosy picture that conjures up!
Here are a few castle shapes . . . copy them or try out some of your own.

One of these could well be Nottingham Castle, where Robin Hood's deadly enemy, the Sheriff of Nottingham, lived. What a brilliant baddy the Sheriff was. If you couldn't pay your taxes he set fire to your house, then strung you up from the nearest tree. Now, that's what I call *bad*!

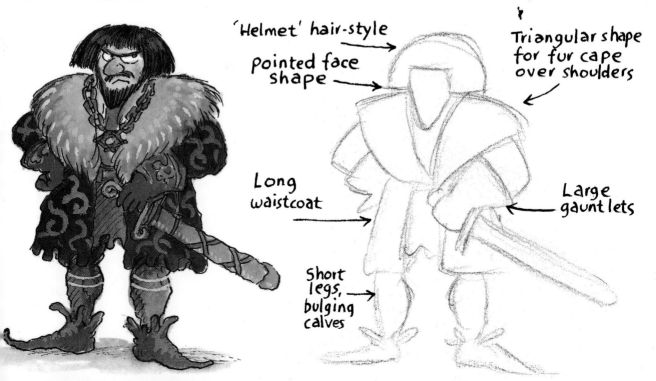

'Helmet' hair-style

pointed face shape

Triangular shape for fur cape over shoulders

Long waistcoat

Large gauntlets

Short legs, bulging calves

Legendary Horrors

F olk tales and legends have lots of wonderful baddies in them too. The ancient Greeks thought up some beauties! Two of the nastiest were the Minotaur and the Medusa.

The Minotaur was half-man, half-bull . . . and totally mad! It roamed the labyrinth in Crete and promptly ate up anyone who dared to venture inside.

'Flower-pot' shaped head ↓

High shoulders →

Thick arms ↘

Barrel-shaped body ↗

Shor thic leg:

The Medusa had the most horrible hair-do in the world . . . . a nest of living snakes! She was so terrifying that anyone who looked at her was immediately turned to stone.

Draw snakes sprouting all round face

← wide nose
big nostrils

Round head

Mouth near chin

I can see right to the tip of your tail!

Who are you calling a dirty, rotten snake?

I can see right up your nose!

I wonder why nobody comes to visit any more?

2+2 = 4
4+4 = 8
8+8 = 16

He's an adder!

I'm a rattle snake.

Dragons didn't have many friends either. Huge, scaly creatures like flying lizards with very bad breath, they thought nothing of having a lightly-toasted village for breakfast followed by roasted town for lunch!

Bat-like wings

Short feathers at top, longer underneath

Round body shape

Ears like wings

Large, round eyes

Front legs have fingers like talons

Head like a crocodile

Tail like a writhing snake

Back legs have toes with claws

Steam and smoke radiating from nostrils

I don't go in much for water myself . . . it has a bad effect on me. (The last time I washed behind my ears one of them fell off!) But I do like the monsters that live in water . . . such as the Kraken from Norwegian folklore, which dragged ships to their doom. Some people think that the Kraken is a giant squid . . . because squid can grow up to 16 metres long!

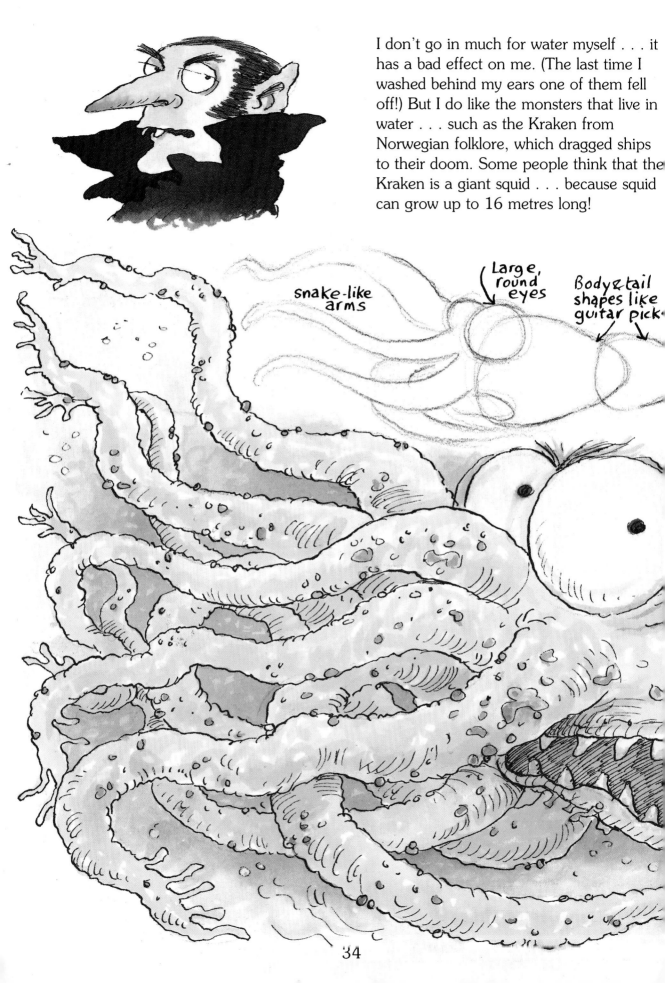

snake-like arms

Large, round eyes

Body & tail shapes like guitar pick

Just before deadtime, I like to do a bit of sketching. I draw mythical monsters from different parts of the world. (It helps to give me nightmares.) Here are a few from my sketchbook. Why not copy them . . . or find some for yourself!

the 'Chimaera' from Greek legend

'Yamantaka' from Indian legend

'Bes' from Egyptian legend

'Kukailimoku' from Oceanic legend

Monster Movie Stars

I love going to the movies. Maybe it's the fact that you have to sit in the dark for hours that appeals to me. I tried bringing my coffin along once but was told that I'd have to sit in a seat like *everybody else.*

My favourite movie baddy is, of course, ME!
Look at my noble profile . . .
those dark, devil-may-care eyes, those sharp fangs.
Even though I say it myself,
I am the best-looking dead person on the planet!

Egg-shaped head

Large, round eyes

Nose like a beak

Cloak collar

Pointed chin

Pointed ears
Cloak collar

Draw me with care . . . or else!

A movie monster that I am particularly fond of is an aristocrat like me . . . King Kong. Unfortunately, he doesn't like to pose for pictures, so here's how to draw his twin brother, Prince Pong.

High shoulders

Head like a coconut

Arms like tree-trunks

Round body shape

Short, thick legs

Big feet

At the end of the movie, King Kong clambered up the side of the Empire State building in New York. (Maybe he thought he'd be able to see his house from the top.) If you draw it at this crazy angle, it will give the impression of tremendous height.

Actually... I was looking for the toilet!

Frankenstein's monster is another movie pal of mine. I always get a nice *buzz* out of seeing him . . . he's got such an *electric* personality!

Use angular shapes...

Rectangular head →

Square shoulders

Long arms

Short sleeves

Wrists showing

Big hands

Big boots

Scar →

Bolts

The Blob was a squishy, runny, yucky monster that could squirm under doors or wriggle through keyholes like melted plastic. It ate up everything in its path . . . rather like a two-year-old at a party!

Here is another use for your slime-painting technique! (Lots of drippy lines painted over with any yucky colour of your choice.)

The Creature from the Black Lagoon is also a good chum. Slimy, slippery and sneaky . . . a perfect pal.

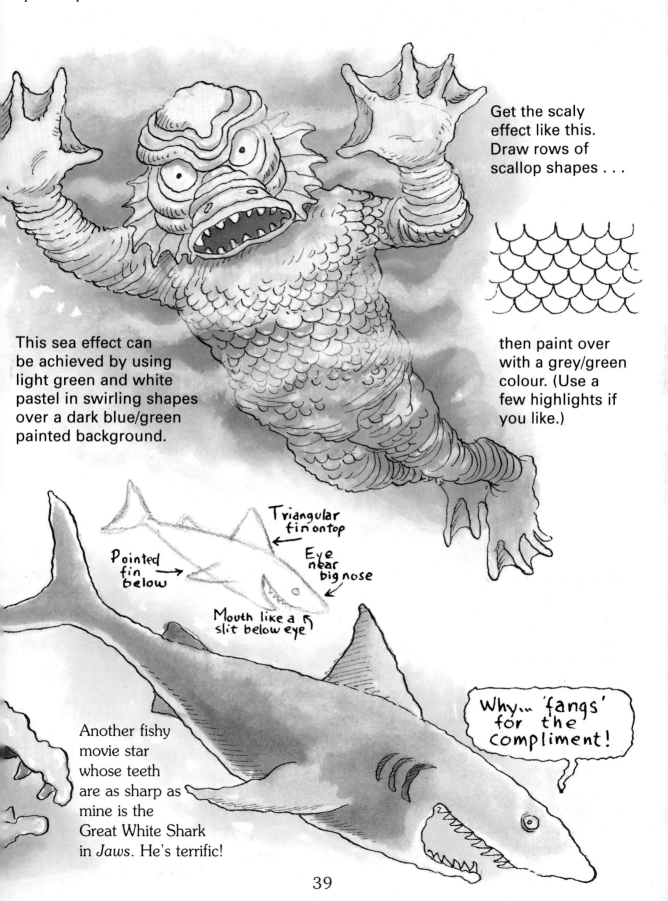

Get the scaly effect like this. Draw rows of scallop shapes . . .

then paint over with a grey/green colour. (Use a few highlights if you like.)

This sea effect can be achieved by using light green and white pastel in swirling shapes over a dark blue/green painted background.

Triangular fin on top

Pointed fin below

Eye near big nose

Mouth like a slit below eye

Another fishy movie star whose teeth are as sharp as mine is the Great White Shark in *Jaws*. He's terrific!

Why... 'fangs' for the compliment!

Skulls and Crossbones

One bunch of baddies that I've always liked drawing are pirates. Cruel, pitiless, slit-your-throat-soon-as-look-at-you types.

The kind of people who will feed their grannies to the sharks for a bit of a laugh on a slow day.

That's the last one, me hearties...we'll have to start using other people's grannies now!

Glass eye
False teeth
Hook

Unfortunately, they were a careless lot, always losing bits of themselves. Eyes . . . teeth . . . legs . . . hands . . . heads. Everything could be replaced . . . except heads!

Wooden leg

Captain Hook, the baddy from Peter Pan, lost his hand when it was bitten off by a gigantic crocodile. The croc liked the taste so much that it was always on the lookout for Hook . . . to make a meal of the rest of him!

Suppertime!

Here's how to draw the revolting reptile.

Jaws like cucumbers

Large, round eyes

Round head

The pirate flag, 'The Jolly Roger', usually looked like this . . . the 'Skull and Crossbones' . . .

but many pirates had their own versions like these. Why not try to design one of your own?

Assorted Rotters

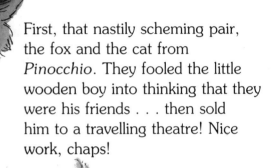

Whenever a baddy takes my fancy from a story, a movie or a play, I get my sketchbook out and do a drawing of the character. Here are a few of those assorted rotters.

First, that nastily scheming pair, the fox and the cat from *Pinocchio*. They fooled the little wooden boy into thinking that they were his friends . . . then sold him to a travelling theatre! Nice work, chaps!

Then there's Baron Greedyguts from the pantomime. He's oily and charming, but his heart is as black as coal and twice as hard. Everyone shouts, 'Boo! Hiss! Look behind you!' as he creeps up on the unsuspecting heroine, but I always shout, 'Don't be silly . . . there's no one there!'

Most people think of Santa Claus when they think of Christmas . . . but not me. He's too happy and jolly. No, I think of Jack Frost . . . the nasty little nipper who pinches your fingers and toes with cold.

'Icicle' spikes

Large, round head

spindly arms

Large eyes

Pointed nose

Small, square body

Long, thin legs

Long, spikey fingers

And sometimes there are baddies who are clever enough to fool everyone into thinking that they are goodies. In the story of Rumpelstiltskin, it's the little goblin man who is always taken for the rotter. But who was it that wanted the straw spun into gold in the first place? And who threatened to cut off the girl's head if she didn't do it? The *king*, that's who! What a brilliantly sneaky, greedy baddy!

Horribly Decent Goodies

And finally, just to show that I am not totally biased, I'll show you how to draw some preposterously good goodies. (Even though it gives me the shudders.)

Robin Hood

Triangular shape for hat

Oval shape for forearm

Rectangle shapes

Body leans forward

Long, thin legs

Sir Galahad

Square shaped torso

'Curved arch' helmet shape

Curved shape

Triangular knee-pads

Shield drawn at slight angle

Peter Pan

'Shield'-shaped head
Pointed ears

Slightly curved, rectangular body

Thin arms

Flying saucer' shaped hat

Shoulders and arms high →

Square face

'Bow' legs →

Fingers spread out

Wyatt Earp

Tarzan

Use oval shapes...

Oval arm shapes

Oval torso →

Oval leg shapes

Oval head

Now quickly, turn this page . . . I'm beginning to feel sick at the sight of all this goodness!

Ah, here we are, back in my superbly slimey studio. I hope you enjoyed the tour.

Remember... keep practising those delightfully disgusting drawings and soon you'll be as good as me... DEAD GOOD!

Yawn! Oh... I think it's time I was tucked up in my cosy coffin...

... but, hold on... where is everyone? And why is it so QUIET?

Usually the rats are howling for their dinner, the Beast is rattling its chains and the bogey-persons are practising unearthly screams...

...so... WHAT'S GOING ON??